RICHMOND PALACE

ITS HISTORY AND ITS PLAN

John Cloake

For Bill and Jean-Anne

with love from John

Richmond

28 May 2002

Richmond Local History Society

FOREWORD

This monograph is being published to celebrate the 500th anniversary of Henry VII's decision to rename his palace of Shene as 'Richmond' after his Yorkshire earldom, a decision which he took when he had (almost) completed his rebuilding of the palace.

The first part recounts briefly the history of the palace and its site. Those who might wish for a more detailed account, with full references to the original sources, should turn to my *Palaces and Parks of Richmond and Kew*, published in two volumes in 1995 and 1996.

The second part sets out how, in a site where very little of the original structure remains, we can produce a reasonably accurate plan of the Tudor palace, as related to the map today. A far more scholarly account of the evidence, both documentary and archaeological, will be forthcoming in the article by Robert Cowie of the Museum of London Archaeological Service in association with myself entitled 'An Archaeological Survey of the Palace of Richmond, Surrey', which is due to be published in the issue of *Post-Mediaeval Archaeology* for the year 2001.

Advances in knowledge and new interpretations are constantly being made. The plan which I first produced in 1975 had evolved by 1986 into my design for the model of Richmond Palace (shown below) which is on show on the Museum of Richmond. Since then, I have discovered that that was inaccurate in some respects in its depiction of the Privy Lodgings building. I think we have now got it about right. The most important new element has been the discovery made in the Medici archives in Florence by Dr Sabine Eiche, an art historian, of a scaled plan showing the Privy Lodgings as the Italian architect Costantino de' Servi proposed to modify them and the palace gardens in 1611. Hitherto we had no significant dimensions for this building and our prime source was the splendid set of mid-16th century drawings by Antonis van Wyngaerde. The model was based largely on these, and even if it is incorrect in some details, I believe that it does still give an excellent impression of the palace. It will figure prominently in the Museum's special exhibition to mark our 500th anniversary.

My thanks are due to Bob Cowie and his colleagues at MOLAS for their permission to reproduce the plan we worked out together, and to Sabine Eiche for the de' Servi plan. But in particular I think we should all be grateful to Henry VII – Richmond is really a much nicer name than Shene.

John Cloake *(September 2000)*

CONTENTS

Front cover: *Detail from Richmond Palace, c.1630 by an unknown artist (Fitzwilliam Museum)*

NOTES

• The geographical axis of the palace buildings from the gate by Richmond Green to the riverside is approximately north-east to south-west. For convenience of description the axis is taken as north-south throughout this publication – a practice which was used in the majority of the original documents.
• The spelling in quotations has been modernised.
• Years, in dates between 1 January and 25 March, before the adoption of the 'new style' calendar in 1752, are shown in the style e.g. January 1509/10

PART ONE

A BRIEF HISTORY OF THE PALACE

chapter 1

The Palaces of Shene

U ntil 500 years ago Richmond in Surrey was called 'Shene'. There were many different ways in which the name was spelled in the middle ages, but the very first historical mention was about 950AD, as 'Sceon' in the will of Theodred, Bishop of London, who owned land there. 'Sceon' means 'of a shed' or 'of a shelter' in Anglo-Saxon English.

At the time of the Domesday survey in 1085, Shene was part of the manor of Kingston, which belonged to the King, and which stretched all the way up to Kew. Kingston was not a large town but it was a place of some importance, where seven Kings of England were crowned in the 10th and early 11th centuries. It was a local administrative centre for both church and state authorities, with a 'minister' church and a royal hall. Though nothing can be proved, it is possible that this royal hall was in fact at Shene on the site of the later royal palaces.

THE ORIGINAL MANOR HOUSE

Early in the 12th century King Henry I detached Shene and Kew from the manor of Kingston and made them into a separate manor of Shene, which he granted to a Norman lord, John Belet. In the 1270s-90s the manor was held by two favourites and close advisers of King Edward I: Robert Burnell, Bishop of Bath and Wells, Chancellor of England, the King's chief minister; and Sir Otto de Grandison, a Swiss knight who had been Edward's companion on a crusade and who was later one of the leaders of the King's army which conquered the remains of the Principality of Wales. He became Constable of Caernarvon and Justiciar of Wales. A few years after the accession of Edward II in 1307, the manor of Shene reverted to the crown: Grandison retired to his castle in Switzerland; another part of the manor was surrendered to the King.

In 1314 King Edward granted the manor house at Shene to found a monastery of Carmelite friars, in thanksgiving for his personal escape after his crushing defeat by the Scots at Bannockburn. But three years later he moved the Carmelites to a new location at Oxford, and regained control of the manor house of Shene. He is known to have visited it several times before his forced abdication in January 1326/7.

Six days after the abdication Shene was granted to Queen Isabella, the wife of Edward II, who had engineered her husband's overthrow and now ran the country with her lover Roger Mortimer in the name of her son the 14-year-old Edward III. Although Edward III asserted himself in 1330, arresting and executing Mortimer and stripping Queen Isabella of many of her lands, the Queen retained Shene until her death in 1358.

EDWARD III'S PALACE

Almost immediately after his mother's death King Edward III began to convert the manor house of Shene into a royal palace. There are many details of the work done there from 1363 to 1368. We know that it stood by the river, that a moat enclosed the lower or 'down court' where the residential buildings were, that the King's Chamber (newly built) was on the upper floor of the side facing the river. We know that a cloister garden was made below the King's old chamber, which had windows 'facing the clock'. We know about the construction of new secondary buildings such as the wardrobe, kitchens and stables and about fireplaces and tiles and glass windows and a candelabrum 'in the shape of five roses'. We know there was a great hall and a chapel, and even that a great barn and a 'hall with two chambers' were purchased from the Archbishop's manor in Wimbledon and moved to Shene; we know that there were farm buildings in an outer or 'over court' outside the moat. But unfortunately there is not enough information to enable us to reconstruct a convincing plan of this first Shene Palace, where King Edward III died in 1377.

Edward III

Edward III's eldest son, the famous 'Black Prince', had died a year before his father, so the heir to the throne was Edward's 10-year-old grandson, Richard II. Young Richard was dominated by his uncles, who arranged a dynastic alliance by marrying Richard in January 1382/3 to Anne of Bohemia, daughter of Holy Roman Emperor Charles IV. The young King and Queen, both in their mid-teens, promptly turned the marriage into a love match. The Palace of Shene was their favourite residence. More work was carried out there, especially by building a summer pavilion on one of the islands in the Thames opposite the palace and providing a new barge and new steps 'for the King's way to the water'. The island provided the young couple with a romantic retreat – to get away for a few hours from the uncles!

Then disaster struck. On Whit Sunday 1394 Queen Anne died at Shene of the plague. Richard was heart-broken; he cursed the place where they had been so happy

Death of Queen Anne at Shene Palace (from Froissart's Chronicles)

but which had now taken her from him. He ordered the complete destruction of Shene Palace – 'as well the houses and buildings in the court within the moat, and the court without the moat, as the houses and buildings in La Neyt [the island] beside the manor'. The demolition of the main palace buildings was carried out, though the farm buildings in the outer court appear to have been spared – and the gardens were still maintained. Though a statue of Queen Anne was erected at Shene on the anniversary of her death, the site was now to remain abandoned for some twenty years.

THE LANCASTRIAN PALACE

Henry IV seems to have had no interest in Shene, but to Henry V, when he came to the throne in March 1412/3, it provided an opportunity. He was anxious to restore some legitimacy to the throne usurped by his father, and to carry out his father's unfulfilled pledge to found three monasteries in expiation of his involvement in the murders of Richard II and Archbishop Scroope. The restoration of the Palace of Shene would help to establish some continuity with the reigns of Edward III and Richard II – and in the royal manors of Shene and Isleworth (which then included all of Twickenham) there was plenty of spare land on which to found monasteries. To carry out 'the King's Great Work' in one single area would achieve economies of effort and cost.

So Henry set about making Shene habitable as quickly as possible. He then commenced building a major new palace there, and founded a Carthusian monastery on royal land a little to the north, a Brigittine convent of Syon in Twickenham just opposite the palace site, and a Celestine monastery at Isleworth. (In the event the Celestine foundation proved abortive; and the Brigittines moved their Syon convent to the abandoned Isleworth site in 1431. It is today the site of Syon House.)

Henry appears to have rejected the idea of simply rebuilding Shene Palace on its old site, which now became an orchard. Instead he planned his major new palace on an adjacent site, still within the old moat, where the gardens had previously been. There were to be new gardens by the riverside outside the eastern arm of the moat; and beyond them was ground where a temporary 'prefabricated' palace could be erected at speed. The King ordered that the buildings of the royal manor house at Byfleet should be taken down and re-erected on this ground at Shene. As they were mostly timber or timber-framed lath and plaster buildings, this was quite easy; only new stone foundations were needed, but a little later a stone chapel was built.

Preparations for the works on the whole complex of projects started in the winter of 1413–14 under the supervision of John Strange, clerk of the King's Works. Stephen Lote, the King's Master Mason, was master-mason for the palace. Materials were gathered from all over England

Henry V

and from the English possessions in France – stone from Caen in Normandy, bricks (still a rarity in England) from Calais, young trees for the new garden from Rouen. Stone came also from Yorkshire and Devon and Surrey (Reigate), lead and plaster from Lancashire, timber from the Surrey woods and glass from London. The cost of shipping bricks from Calais proved so expensive that a brick kiln using local clay was set up at Petersham. The royal house at Sutton in Chiswick, where some of the materials from Shene had been reused in Richard II's time, was now in its turn demolished and its materials cannibalised for use at Shene.

Work on 'the new manor called Byfleet within the manor of Shene' was given priority. In the years up to 1419 expenditure on Byfleet was £5,815 while that on 'the foundations of the [new] manor of Shene' was less than half that – only £2,368.

Byfleet seems to have been a complete royal complex in itself, with King's ward and Queen's ward and a chapel, and it was decorated with a 'great antelope carved in wood' over the kitchen and a further 80 antelopes and swans carved by Peter Kervour for the King's parlour and chamber. Lions and fleurs-de-lys adorned the beams and cornices. By the time of Henry V's death in 1422, the Byfleet complex must have been more or less finished; but work on the new main building was still far from complete.

At the time of Henry's death, his heir, Henry VI, was only a one-year-old baby. Henry V's brothers, John Duke of Bedford and Humphrey Duke of Gloucester reigned in his stead. Though Bedford was nominally Regent, he was fighting the war in France and Gloucester acted as 'Protector of the Realm' in England. Work at Shene was suspended until 1429 when the King's Council ousted Gloucester from his 'protectorate' and arranged for the coronation of the eight-year-old King. This event led to a decision to resume work at Shene to complete the new palace building. This had been achieved by 1439, but then there was another burst of building activity occasioned by the King's marriage in 1445 to Margaret of Anjou. Some work was done at Byfleet as well as in the main new building, but the principal activity at this time was the extension of the palace by building out onto the Green, with lodgings round a new outer court, a new gateway and a new walled extension to the gardens.

This brought the site of the palace to its full later extent, and it is possible to see in the arrangement achieved by 1450 an almost exact precursor of the plan of the later Tudor palace, with its great outer court, a second smaller court with hall and chapel on the landward side of the moat, and then the main building with the royal apartments ('the Privy Lodgings') standing towards the river, enclosed (together with the former palace site, now the great orchard) by the line of the old moat. To the east were the new gardens and then Byfleet, surrounded by a moat of its own. The main palace building probably had a square plan round a small central court, with corner towers and smaller projecting towers spaced along the outer walls. The walls by this time would have been pierced with large windows – no arrowslits, even if they were crowned by battlements. A 'castle' was now designed more as a residence than as a fortress, and the rooms could be well lit.

The civil wars in the latter part of Henry VI's reign prevented any further work at Shene; and in 1466 King Edward IV granted the manor and palace to his Queen, Elizabeth Woodville. It was visited in 1480 by William of Worcester who noted some useful dimensions.

In 1483 Edward IV died and the throne was wrested from the young King Edward V by his uncle Richard Duke of York (Richard III). Two years later Henry Tudor, Earl of Richmond, defeated Richard at the Battle of Bosworth Field and became King as Henry VII. In 1486 he reclaimed Shene from Queen Elizabeth Woodville, who became his mother-in-law when, in January of that year, he married Edward IV's daughter Elizabeth of York.

chapter 2

The fire and the rebuilding

THE FIRE

Soon after he recovered Shene Palace King Henry VII embarked on an extensive programme of repairs and alterations. Full details of the work are not known, but two new large towers were built (one at least by the chapel), and it would seem that the entire palace was probably re-roofed with lead. For some reason the Prior of Shene Charterhouse was in charge of, or at least paymaster for, this operation.

In 1497 the King and his court came to spend Christmas at Shene. In the night of 23 December a fire broke out in the King's lodging. It raged for three hours before it could be extinguished. According to one chronicler: 'Much and great part of the old building of that place was burned' along with 'many notable and rich jewels and other things of superabundant value'.

The Milanese Ambassador reported to his Duke:

> '*The night before Christmas Eve a fire broke out in the place where His Majesty was staying with the Queen and the court, by accident and not by malice, catching a beam, about the ninth hour of the night. It did a great deal of harm and burned the chapel, except two large towers recently*

The fire at Shene Palace, an imaginative illustration to Holinshed's Chronicle

Henry VII

erected by His Majesty. The damage is estimated at 60,000 ducats. The King does not attach much importance to the loss by this fire, seeing it was not due to malice. He purposes to rebuild the chapel all in stone and much finer than before.'

It is indeed somewhat uncertain how much of the old structure was destroyed, apart from the chapel. The King and court were still residing at Shene a month later and were there again in the summer of 1498 – but they probably moved into the 'Byfleet' complex, which might have been spared from the fire because of the garden and moat lying between it and the main palace.

There may well have been enough of the old 'Privy Lodgings' building left to have made it possible to use this as a basis for the new building that Henry VII now resolved upon. As we shall see, the Tudor 'Privy Lodgings' building had a plan that closely resembled that of castles built in the first half of the 15th century.

Although there was by this time a resident clerk of works at Shene, the extent of the new building works called for special arrangements. The former Prior of Shene Charterhouse, who had been appointed Bishop of Llandaff, was brought back to take charge again; and when he died in 1499 Sir William Tyler, a former Comptroller of the King's Works who owned property in Shene village, took over from him. Under them, Nicholas Grey was the local clerk of works and was succeeded in that capacity by Henry Smythe in 1505. We do not know the names of the master mason or the master bricklayer – for hardly any of the works accounts have survived – but the master carpenter was Thomas Bynks, Master of the Carpenters' Company in London in 1495–97 and 1500–02.

Most of the work of rebuilding was completed by 1501. The Great Chronicle of London records:

> 'The King, having finished much of his new building at his manor of Shene and again furnished and repaired that before was perished with fire ... [commanded] that from then forth on it should be named his manor of Rychemount and not Shene.'

The renaming was of course in honour of the Yorkshire earldom bestowed on Henry's father and by which title he himself had been known before he came to the throne. But one contemporary chronicler said it was 'Rich mount' because it had cost so much!

For the next generation Richmond Palace was the show place of the kingdom. The first opportunity to show it off to admiring foreign guests came when King Henry's eldest son, Prince Arthur, was married at St Paul's Cathedral to the Princess

Catherine of Aragon, daughter of King Ferdinand and Queen Isabella of Spain, in November 1501. After the festivities Henry brought the court and the Spanish guests to Richmond. One of the heralds wrote a detailed account both of the new palace and the festivities there, describing the palace as 'the bright and shining star of building; the mirror and pattern of all palaces of delight, commodity and pleasure'.

THE MAIN BUILDINGS

In the description of the palace that follows, all the phrases and sentences in inverted commas (not otherwise attributed) are taken from the herald's account.

Although the usual means of access to Richmond Palace would have been by river, on this occasion the guests had disembarked at Mortlake from the procession of 60 decorated barges and had come on horseback to the main landward gate of the palace. There 300 gentlemen and yeomen of the guard were waiting with torches to light them in. The 'strong gates of double timber and heart of oak ... crossed with bars of iron' stood in a 'strong and mighty brick wall' facing the Green, 'beset with towers in its each corner and angle and also in its middle way'. Through the gate one entered 'a fair, large and broad court, raised and banked in the middle for the rain slough having its channels and voidings', around which were brick galleries containing apartments and offices for the courtiers and officers of the household. On the left was the wardrobe, where not only clothing but the soft furnishings of the palace were kept when not in use.

At the far end of this first court was a three-storey gateway, this time of stone, decorated with the stone figures of two trumpeters, which led into the smaller central court of the palace, with the chapel on the left, the great hall on the right and a fountain in the centre:

> 'a conduit and cistern of stone, four-square, craftily made, with goodly springs and cocks running in its four quarters beneath, that at the will of the drawers of the water open and are closed again.' [Taps were a novelty

Wyngaerde: looking over the Great Court and Fountain Court to the Privy Lodgings

to be remarked upon.] *'In the upper part there are lions and dragons, and other goodly beasts; and in the middle certain branches of red roses out of which flowers and roses is evermore running and course of clean and most pure water into the cistern beneath.'*

The Great Hall, on the right (west) side of this 'Fountain Court', stood on an undercroft which had an entrance from the main court. The stone building rose to a height of some 45 feet and was 100 feet long internally. A large domed and louvred central lantern let out the smoke from a central hearth, but there were also two chimneys serving fireplaces at each end, which were no doubt placed on the dais and by the screens. Between the windows were 'pictures of the noble Kings of this realm', especially the notable warriors including King Henry VII himself. These 'pictures' were probably the statues mentioned in the 1649 Parliamentary Survey (see p.27). The chief glory of the Hall was, however, its roof: 'of timber, not beamed nor braced, but proper knots, craftily carved, joined and shut together with mortices and pinned, hanging pendant from the said roof towards the ground and floor, after the most new invention and craft of the pure practice of geometry'.

The Chapel, also built of stone, on the other side of 'Fountain Court', was 'well paved, glazed and hung with cloth of Arras, the body and the choir with cloth of gold, and the altars set with many relics, jewels and rich plate'. Here there were more 'pictures of Kings of this realm', this time of those more famed for saintly than for military qualities. The 'roof is ceiled and white, limed and checkered with timber lozengewise, painted with colour of azure, having between every check a red rose of gold or a portcullis.' At the sides of the Chapel were private closets for the King and for the Queen and the senior ladies of the court.

THE PRIVY LODGINGS

The Hall and the Chapel were joined by a gallery across the southern side of the 'Fountain Court', from which a bridge spanned the old mediaeval moat to give access to the Privy Lodgings. This latter was an almost square building, with just a small internal court to give light to the inner rooms. It was mostly of three storeys, and its outer walls were liberally furnished with towers: one at each corner, four or five along each side. Most of these towers were topped with elaborate 'pepper-pot' domes, set within battlements and often ringed with delicate stone strap-work, King's beasts or other ornamentation. At the south-west corner (and probably at the north-west also) was a circular staircase tower; at the north-east, the great 'canted tower' which the 1649 survey described as 'a chief ornament unto the whole fabric'. The tower stood four storeys high, above a cellar, with a large room on each floor, and a grand staircase of 120 steps. At the south-east corner it seems that an original tower was partially covered by a two-storey building projecting out to the eastern arm of the moat, and serving as a watergate. The main landing stage would have been just outside this building.

The precise arrangement of rooms within the Privy Lodgings at this time is not known; it is clear that both the King's and the Queen's apartments were on the east-

Wyngaerde: The Privy Lodgings seen from the river

ern side overlooking the gardens, so it is likely that the King's chambers were on the middle floor and the Queen's above – the lower floor being given over mainly to the officers of the household. There would have been a guardroom, of course, and there were 'pleasant dancing chambers' and 'secret closets'. All were 'beset with badges of gold' and 'hung with rich and costly cloths of Arras'.

THE DOMESTIC OFFICES (see illustration p.46)

The kitchen and domestic offices were on the outside of the moat, on the western side of the Great Hall. There was a special 'privy kitchen' for the royal family, and a huge 'livery kitchen' for the rest – its pyramidal, louvred roof standing almost as high as the Great Hall or the turrets on the privy lodgings. There was a pantry and a pastry, a flesh larder and a fish larder, a poultry house and a scalding house and an ale buttery. A large communal 'house of office' [lavatory] stood where it could discharge into the moat. There were special rooms for the cooks near the kitchens; and there was a hostel called 'the Woodyard Lodging', a half-timbered building beside the wood and coal stores, near the side gate into what is now Old Palace Lane.

This lane on the western side of the palace led down from the Green, past the Clerk of Works' yard and the woodyard, and then beside the western arm of the moat, to the palace wharf on which stood a crane for the unloading of freight for the court. It ran through an open funnel of land, widening out towards the river end, called 'Crane Piece'. The old royal park established in the time of Henry VI was on its west side.

THE GARDENS AND THE GALLERIES

Between this western arm of the moat and the Privy Lodgings lay the Great Orchard, which, at the time of the Parliamentary Survey in 1649, had 223 fruit trees planted in the centre and another 170 round the walls. On the eastern side of the Wardrobe, the Chapel and the Privy Lodgings were the Privy Gardens (see illustration p.48):

> *'Most fair and pleasant gardens, with royal knots, alleyed and herbed;*
> *many marvellous beasts, as lions, dragons and such other of divers kinds,*

properly fashioned and carved in the ground, right well sounded and com-
passed in with lead; with many vines, seeds and strange fruit ... kept and
nourished with much labour and diligence. In the lower end of this garden
be pleasant galleries and houses to disport in, at chess, tables, dice, cards,
billiards; bowling alleys, butts for archers and goodly tennis plays – as well
to use the said plays and disports as to behold them so disporting.'

These galleries round the gardens, of two storeys, open below and closed above, were of half-timbered construction. They swept round, in a series of obtuse-angled turns in their southern part, to the moat (where they were linked in 1517 directly to the Privy Lodgings block by a bridge over the moat). There was a tower at their mid-point (linked to the Friary Chapel, see below) and another at their northern end, where they turned inwards to run behind the open tennis court (which stood at the eastern end of the wall facing the Green). A short spur was later built past the eastern end of the tennis court to a half-timbered Banqueting House constructed in 1534. The galleries were a new feature in English palace architecture. There were already somewhat similar features in some palaces in Burgundy (and Prior Ingleby of Shene might well have seen them when visiting the Charterhouse at Bruges); but another influence which may have suggested the idea was the great cloister at the Charterhouse itself. The galleries were not constructed until 1503–05; but in July 1506 part of them collapsed just after the King and the Prince had been walking in them. Bynks, the master-carpenter, was cast into prison, and the whole of his work in the palace subjected to a stringent quality inspection. The repairs, not only to the galleries but also to the roofs of the Hall and Chapel 'through Bynks' faults', were entrusted to a new master-carpenter John Squier.

THE FRIARY

It was therefore not until about 1507 that the new palace was really completed. But, in the meantime, 'Byfleet' was in the process of being converted to a new use. About 1501 King Henry had founded at Richmond a new house for Observant Friars. They were Franciscans who 'observed' the reforms of their order instituted in 1421 – and Henry was a strong admirer of the order. He suppressed four house of 'Conventuals' (those who resisted the reforms) and gave them to Observants. He gave his patronage to the house at Greenwich Palace recently founded by Edward IV – and now he matched this by giving to his own new foundation the buildings of Byfleet. They were in quite good repair; they included a chapel; they would need some, but not a lot of, work to make them suitable. A contract was signed with three master craftsmen: Bynks, Henry Redman, a mason, and Robert Nevill, a bricklayer. The first payment was made in May 1502 and what appeared to be the final payment was made in July 1506. But it was only in March 1509 that a payment was made to the clerk of works Henry Smythe 'for full finishing of the Friars at Richmond'.

chapter 3

The Palace in Tudor times

Henry VII made much use of his new Richmond Palace. Although Prince Arthur had died within five months of his marriage Henry was determined to hang on to the alliance with Spain and the Empire and proposed to betroth the widowed Catherine to Arthur's younger brother Henry, the new Prince of Wales. When a papal dispensation permitting this had been received, Catherine was formally allotted apartments in Richmond Palace while her father-in-law negotiated (for years, but in vain) with her father for a second dowry.

In the meantime, another dynastic marriage, which was in the long term to be of much greater significance, was achieved by the betrothal of King Henry's daughter Margaret to King James IV of Scotland. As the Queen, who was staying at Richmond while expecting another child, was unwell, it was decided to hold the betrothal ceremonies there. There were great celebrations (with jousting on the Green) in January 1502/3 when the Archbishop of Glasgow, the senior Scottish guest, conducted the ceremony of betrothal in the Queen's Great Chamber, King James being represented by the Earl of Bothwell as proxy. A week later the Queen, who had returned to the Tower of London, was delivered of a daughter, but both she and the baby died.

Princess Catherine's eldest sister Joanna, now Queen of Castile, and her new husband Philip of Burgundy, paid an unplanned visit to Richmond in February 1505/6 after the ship in which they were sailing from the Netherlands to Spain was driven ashore on the English coast by a storm. Again there were celebrations and jousting. In September 1506 Philip died. Henry VII at once offered to marry the widow Joanna, but settled instead for a plan to betroth his ten-year old daughter Mary to Philip's six-year old son Charles who was heir to both Aragon and Castile. It took two years of diplomatic negotiations but in December 1508 the betrothal was duly celebrated at Richmond with the usual banquets and jousts.

Four months later, on 21 April 1509, King Henry died in his Palace of Richmond.

KING HENRY VIII'S ACCESSION

The new king, Henry VIII, at once demonstrated that the delay over his actual marriage to Catherine of Aragon was not of his making. Although King Ferdinand had steadfastly refused to produce a second dowry, Henry now married his fiancée of six years' standing within seven weeks of his father's death and two weeks before his own coronation. There were great festivities and more tournaments when the royal couple spent the Christmas season at Richmond in 1509 and 1510. Catherine had had a still-born daughter in January 1509/10, but on 1 January 1510/1 she was delivered, at Richmond, of a son. The boy was christened Henry in the chapel of the Richmond Friary on 5 January, and the event was celebrated with a splendid pageant at the palace. In early February there was a special tournament – and more pageants – at

Westminster. Then on 22 February the infant prince, who had been left to nurse at Richmond, died there. Catherine was to bear another son in 1513, but he lived for a few days only. The only child of the marriage who survived infancy was Princess Mary, born in February 1515/6.

Henry, in collusion with King Ferdinand and the Emperor Maximilian, had become involved in war with France in 1512 and was personally leading his army in the field there in 1513 when King James IV of Scotland launched an attack on his brother-in-law's country in support of the 'auld alliance' between Scotland and France. James's army was cut to pieces by the English at Flodden Field, and James himself was killed. The English commander brought his body down to the English court, and left it in the Shene Charterhouse, while Queen Catherine wrote from Richmond to Henry to ask what should be done with it. King Henry wrote to the Pope asking permission to give King James a fitting and Christian burial, for he had been excommunicated for the attack on England. The Pope agreed, but for some reason the ceremony never took place and the body, embalmed and wrapped in lead, just remained unburied in a room at Shene. Its ultimate fate is unknown, but it must surely have been discreetly disposed of before the arrival of King James VI of Scotland on the English throne in 1603!

Henry VIII

In 1514 both Ferdinand and Maximilian withdrew from the war against the French who were suing for peace. When Henry proposed that the marriage between Charles and his sister Mary should now be celebrated, Ferdinand stalled. The French King, Louis XII, had just been left a widower and the French now made peace overtures to Henry, proposing that Louis should marry Princess Mary. Vexed with Ferdinand's behaviour, Henry agreed. Mary, who wanted neither the young Charles of Castile nor the aged Louis of France, but rather her sweetheart Charles Brandon, Duke of Suffolk, reluctantly agreed on the understanding that she would be free to marry Suffolk when Louis died. The marriage was celebrated in October 1514. Less than three months later Louis died. Henry had some hope of remarrying Mary to the new King of France, Louis's son, Francis I. Such ideas were dashed when Henry learned, to his great annoyance, that Mary had promptly married the Duke of Suffolk who had been sent as ambassador to congratulate Francis on his succession.

The formal treaty of peace between England and France was signed at Richmond Palace on 9 April 1515. A few days later ambassadors from Venice were entertained at

Richmond on St George's day when the ceremonies of the Order of the Garter were held there. For some years Richmond rather than Windsor appears to have been the meeting place of the Order.

HAMPTON COURT AND CARDINAL WOLSEY

But now Richmond began to see the growth nearby of a rival palace. Cardinal Wolsey, now Archbishop of York and the King's chief counsellor, acquired a lease of the manor of Hampton Court and began to build there a sumptuous palace, larger than the King's at Richmond. By May 1516 the work was sufficiently advanced for him to invite the King and Queen to dine there. For the time being however Henry continued to make much use of Richmond – even more than usual because of repeated out-breaks of plague in London – and he had various small works under-taken, such as the building of the new bridge over the moat in 1517 which connect-ed his apartments directly with the garden galleries. The greatest excitement for the Richmond population in the next few years was the visit in 1522 of Charles of Castile, now King of Spain, and recently elected as Holy Roman Emperor. With a retinue of 208 noblemen and gentlemen, 100 household officers and 1710 servants the resources of Richmond must have been severely stretched!

By 1552, Wolsey's sumptuous establishment at Hampton Court was beginning to arouse both popular criticism and royal envy. And Catherine's failure to present Henry with a living male heir was beginning to focus Henry's already roving eye. Henry had had an affair with Elizabeth Blount who had borne him a son Henry Fitzroy, created Duke of Richmond in 1525 at the age of six, and another with Mary Boleyn. His eye now fell on her younger sister Anne. Though Henry continued to use Richmond Palace, Catherine was increasingly left there on her own with her daugh-ter Mary, leading the Spanish ambassador to refer to Richmond Palace as 'the Queen's Palace'.

About 1524 or 1525 Wolsey made some sort of arrangement with Henry whereby the rights of present use when he wished and the eventual reversion of ownership of Hampton Court were granted to the King, while Wolsey was allowed to make some personal use of Richmond. The precise terms of this arrangement were, perhaps deliberately, obscure. Wolsey now referred to Hampton Court as 'Your Grace's manour', but the King wrote courteously asking Wolsey to move out of his house when he wanted to use it for a few days. It does seem however that Henry managed to saddle Wolsey with the costs of upkeep of both!

THE PALACE AND KING HENRY'S MARRIAGES

The King's breach with his wife developed rapidly from 1527 to 1529. Wolsey did his best in the King's cause, but he could not get the Pope to agree to consider a divorce unless Henry presented himself in Rome. There was no way Henry would accept such a demand. The breach with Rome began as a series of anti-papal laws were enacted. In October 1529 Wolsey was dismissed as Chancellor. Catherine was ordered to remain in retirement at Richmond Palace while Anne Boleyn took her place at court. Two years later Richmond was appointed as a home for Princess Mary. However, by 1533 Thomas More, who had succeeded Wolsey as Chancellor and who was opposed to the divorce, had himself been replaced by the tough Thomas Cromwell and Archbishop Warham had been replaced as Archbishop of Canterbury by the compliant Thomas Cranmer. In May 1533 Cranmer pronounced the divorce of Henry and Catherine and on the following day he confirmed the marriage of Henry and Anne, which had been celebrated secretly the previous winter. In September 1533 Anne's daughter Elizabeth was born – and her elder half-sister Mary was now declared illegitimate, stripped of her title of Princess to become a mere dependent of the household of Princess Elizabeth.

Henry and Anne were frequently at Richmond together, and more improvements were carried out there. Then Anne fell from favour and was executed for adultery in May 1536. Henry married Jane Seymour and was reconciled, at Richmond, with his daughter Mary who again made her home mainly at Richmond Palace.

Queen Jane died at Richmond Palace in October 1537, two weeks after giving birth to a son Edward at Hampton Court. Fifteen months later the King married Anne of Cleves.The marriage was swiftly agreed to be a failure and Anne accepted a divorce and a handsome settlement. This included the grant not just of Richmond Palace, but of the manors of Richmond, Petersham and Ham. How much use Anne made of Richmond Palace is not known, but Henry came there no more after one quick visit to thank her for her acquiescence in the divorce. After Henry's death in 1547 Anne handed back Richmond Palace and the manors to the young Edward VI. A major programme of repairs was promptly put in hand.

Edward was a sickly youth and it seemed unlikely that he would live to marry and produce an heir. The grandees who now ran the country plotted to ensure that the Catholic Princess Mary should not succeed him. Elizabeth had been declared illegit-imate when her mother was executed. They chose instead Jane Grey, granddaughter of Charles Brandon and Princess Mary. Her father, Henry Grey, who had been cre-ated Duke of Suffolk on the death of Brandon's sons, had his home in the remains of the Charterhouse of Shene. The Duke of Northumberland, the Lord Protector, had taken over the mansion at Syon, and married his son Guilford Dudley to Jane. Together they planned to put Jane on the throne as soon as Edward died. Edward himself was persuaded to name Jane as his successor. But just nine days after the death of Edward and the proclamation of Queen Jane, the people of the country – at least those in London and the South-East – had made it clear that they wanted Mary. Northumberland and Suffolk caved in and proclaimed Mary as Queen.

QUEEN MARY

Mary set out at once for London and after spending a couple of weeks at the Tower she moved to Richmond, where she issued a proclamation calling for toleration for both forms of worship and where she received a Spanish embassy proposing that she should marry King Phillip of Spain. She was averse to the idea of marriage, but per-suaded of the need to produce a Catholic heir. Further negotiations took place at

Richmond at Christmas 1553 and the deal was concluded. But there was much popular opposition to the idea of a Spanish marriage. Then in January Sir Thomas Wyatt raised his rebellion and marched on London. His rebellion failed, but it was a turning point. Mary, who had up to then been merciful to the earlier plotters, was now persuaded to execute Jane and Guilford Dudley and Suffolk. Princess Elizabeth was accused of complicity, and held at the Tower, then briefly at Richmond, and finally under house arrest at Woodstock in Oxfordshire.

In July Philip landed at Southampton. The marriage was celebrated at Winchester. On the way back to London they spent a week at Richmond Palace. Mary and Cardinal Pole, a distant cousin of the Queen and newly appointed Papal Legate and Archbishop of Canterbury, now set about restoring the old religion – and even some of the monasteries including Shene and Syon; and they became ruthless in this cause. But it soon became evident that Mary was not going to produce an heir; and Phillip, who was a pragmatist, insisted that they must just accept that Elizabeth would probably be the next Queen of England, that they should treat her honourably, and try to win her to and keep her in the faith. In July 1557 Mary gave a great party at Richmond, and Princess Elizabeth was, if not the guest of honour, at least an honoured guest brought down from London in a specially decorated barge.

Mary made full use of Richmond Palace. Though the Tudor courts were always nomadic, usually staying in one place only for two or three weeks before moving on to another, Mary established a record when she stayed at Richmond for two and a half months in the summer of 1555. In 1558 she visited Richmond in both spring and summer but on both occasions fever forced her return to London. On 17 November 1558 she died. Cardinal Pole died the same evening.

QUEEN ELIZABETH AND THE PALACE

Within six months of Elizabeth's succession the Protestant religion had been fully restored by parliamentary legislation. But the other question that most troubled Parliament was that the Queen should marry and bear an heir. She told them that she would live and die a virgin – but could they believe this when they saw the evident closeness of her friendship with Lord Robert Dudley, whom she made Master of the Horse, to whom she gave a mansion and lands at Kew, close to Richmond which she now began to use frequently? At Richmond and Kew, at Brentford and in London, rumours of the romance were generated and flourished. Dudley's wife was unwell, and the Spanish ambassador was convinced that the Queen and Robert were just waiting for her to die in order to marry. When she did die in 1560 it was in suspicious circumstances that put paid to any such possibility, though Robert was officially held to be blameless. Their close relationship continued however until his death in 1588. Whatever other favourites she had, he was always the one to whom she returned.

Richmond Palace underwent a change in appearance in 1565–7 when much of the elaborate decoration around the pepper-pot domes was taken down because it had become dangerous. Further works in Queen Elizabeth's time included repair of the

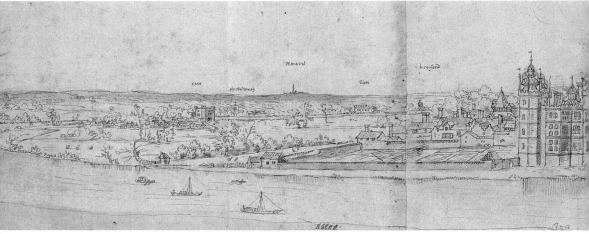

Richmond Palace from the river by Wyngaerde

garden galleries and replacement of windows, a new livery kitchen and a new land-ing stage in the 1570s, the building of a stage for plays in 1588–89, more repairs and much repainting, renovation of the fountain, another new landing stage, a new room at the main gate for the porters, and the installation of a flushing water-closet (invented by the Queen's godson Sir John Harington) in the 1590s.

Much of the history of Richmond Palace during the reign of Elizabeth is a mat-ter of frequent royal visits, two or three times a year, of the reception and entertain-ment of foreign ambassadors, and in later years – especially at Christmas and Shrovetide – the performance of plays by the several companies of actors maintained by leading members of the court, including that in which Shakespeare was a mem-ber. A few incidents do, however, stand out from this routine.

A secret treaty was signed at Richmond in September 1562 between Elizabeth and the leaders of the French Huguenots, by which Elizabeth hoped to regain Calais by aiding the Huguenots. But all that the English army brought back from their adven-ture in France was the plague. Meanwhile Elizabeth herself had almost died of small-pox, and the question of her marriage and the succession became again a matter of national concern. She could not bring herself to acknowledge that her heir apparent was Mary Queen of Scots – another granddaughter of Henry VII – but devised the curious scheme of marrying Robert Dudley, whom she made Earl of Leicester, to Mary. That idea was opposed by Dudley himself – and then Mary fell in love with the young Earl of Darnley, married him, and produced a son James, who became the next in line to the English throne.

Elizabeth managed to keep both potential suitors and her loyal subjects' concerns at bay by an elaborate game of apparent flirtations (political usually, rather than per-sonal). Many of the suitors came to Richmond in person, others sent high-ranking emissaries: the King of Sweden sent his sister, the Emperor (on behalf of his son the Archduke Charles) a special ambassador. The most ardent suitor was however Francis, Duke of Alençon and later Duke of Anjou, brother of the French King.

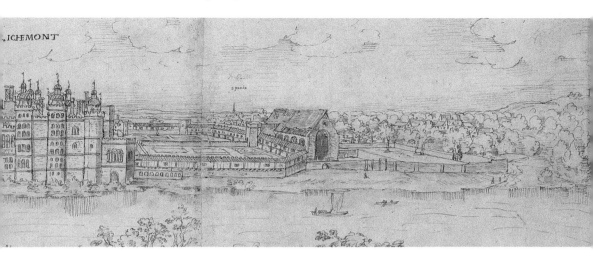

Elizabeth was quite taken by him. Negotiations in 1572 were aborted as a result of the savage repression of the Huguenots that followed the massacre of St Bartholomew, but were resumed some years later. In 1579 the Duke of Anjou visited Elizabeth secretly at Greenwich, and she was captivated. But when she put the question of approving a possible marriage to her Council, they would only say that they could not advise in favour, but would not oppose if it were the Queen's wish. She told Francis that she must wait to win more general support.

In 1581 the Duke of Anjou returned, quite openly this time, to visit her at Richmond. While he stayed in the palace, the Bell Inn, the Red Lyon Inn and two other houses were requisitioned to house his suite. He was confident of success, and the Queen exchanged rings with him, kissed him in public and told the French ambassador that 'the Duke of Anjou shall be my husband'. But then she changed her mind, and told Francis that she must sacrifice her personal happiness for her people's welfare, and could not marry him. He remained in England for another three months, being feasted and banqueted, and when he finally departed the Queen went with him as far as Canterbury and wept as she said goodbye. She wrote to him frequently but never saw him again. He died three years later.

In 1586 Philip of Spain, fed up with the constant English raids on Spanish shipping and ports and given an additional moral *casus belli* by the execution of Mary Queen of Scots, decided to invade and subdue England. The transport of a large army from the Spanish Netherlands was to be protected by the Armada, a great fleet of warships that were to seize control of the English Channel. A preemptive strike by Sir Francis Drake delayed the Armada's departure from Cadiz, but eventually it sailed at the end of May 1588. On 19 July it was sighted off the Lizard. Elizabeth had moved to Richmond a fortnight earlier, and it was in Richmond Palace that the defence of the country against the threatened invasion was planned.

For Elizabeth the triumph and relief of the Armada's destruction, by the English fleet and by gales, was clouded by the death of the Earl of Leicester. His place was

Elizabeth I, from the 'Armada' portrait by Gower

now to be taken by his stepson: the young and handsome, impetuous Robert Devereux, Earl of Essex .

In the 1580s the Queen largely gave up the annual 'progresses' during which she had toured the country within comparatively easy reach of London, staying with (and thereby impoverishing, but sometimes knighting or ennobling) the noblemen and rich gentry. She now spent more time in the palaces in and close to London – and especially liked Richmond in winter – probably because it was more compact and therefore easier to heat. It was her 'warm winter box, to shelter her old age'.

QUEEN ELIZABETH'S LAST DAYS

The Queen, though in reasonably good health, was becoming conscious of her age. In 1597 Dr Rudd, the Bishop of St David's, incurred her wrath by a sermon given in the Richmond Palace chapel in which he was rash enough to discourse on mystical numbers including 63 – which was the Queen's age. The French ambassador noted that she 'walked daily on Richmond Green with greater spirit and activity than could be expected of her years'. But she was deeply distressed by Essex's abortive little rebellion – and subsequent execution – in February 1600/1.

In October 1602 the court was at Richmond, 'where the Queen finds herself so well that she will not easily remove'. She had to return to London in November but planned to spend Christmas at Richmond. State business and various entertainments detained her in London and it was not until 21 January that she finally arrived back in Richmond 'in very foul and wet weather'. She had a cold, but seemed to throw it off; then she fell prey to it again at the beginning of March. While her resistance was lowered, her favourite lady-in-waiting and kinswoman, the Countess of Nottingham, died quite suddenly – and the Queen was grievously afflicted. On 23 March 1602/3 she died in Richmond Palace.

There is a quite unfounded but picturesque story that when Elizabeth died, her ring was dropped from the window of the 'death chamber' – above the gateway – to a rider below who galloped with it to King James of Scotland, her successor on the English throne. It is obvious nonsense to think that she would have died in a room which had only been built a year or two before as accommodation for the porters at the main gate. The true story is just as compelling. The horseman was Robert Carey, Warden of the Middle March on the Scottish border, brother of the Countess of Nottingham, of Lady Scrope (another of the Queen's ladies) and of Lord Hunsdon, the Lord Chamberlain. They were all grandchildren of Mary Boleyn, and so Elizabeth's first cousins once removed. (There is some reason to believe that Henry VIII was their grandfather, which would make them Elizabeth's nephews and nieces.) Robert Carey left a first-hand account of how he came to take the ring to James, in the belief that it would establish his fortune to be the first to bring the news to the new King.

After days in which the Queen refused to take to her bed though obviously very unwell, she was finally persuaded to lie down in her chamber. She lost the power of speech. Carey had left the palace for his lodging, but, as he had arranged, was notified at once of the Queen's death. He had difficulty in gaining admission to the palace because the Privy Council had ruled that no one should go in or out, but was finally admitted on the say-so of a member of the Council. But then, having established that the Queen was indeed dead (and having presumably been given the ring – perhaps by his sister Lady Scrope), he was not allowed out. He dragged his brother the Lord Chamberlain out of bed, and the latter ordered the porter to let Carey out. He got no further than London that night and only avoided arrest by the Council there next morning as the result of a warning from a friend in the Council. He rode off at once to the north. On the third day of his journey he was thrown from his horse and a blow to the head from a hoof compelled him to go much slower. King James had gone to bed by the time Carey reached Edinburgh, but he was admitted, greeted the King by his title 'England, Scotland, France and Ireland' and produced the 'blue ring from a fair lady' as proof of his credentials.

Queen Elizabeth's last progress was by river from Richmond to Whitehall, where she lay in state for a month, before her state funeral in Westminster Abbey.

chapter 4

The Palace from 1603 to 1660

Henry, Prince of Wales at Richmond

Shortly after his accession to the throne King James, who loved hunting, decided that Richmond must have a bigger and better park. This was created, to the north and west of the palace, by adding much of the former Charterhouse land and some remaining demense land to the smaller park made by Henry VI, and finally by adding an extra 33 acres which the King purchased from the local inhabitants. This park, completed by 1606, with a hunting lodge at its centre, is today represented by the Old Deer Park and the southern part of Kew Gardens.

RICHMOND PALACE AS THE SEAT OF THE PRINCE OF WALES

The King decided that Richmond Palace should be used primarily as a home for his children. Prince Henry, the eldest, and Prince Charles were installed there with their tutors while their sister Princess Elizabeth was given into the charge of Lord and Lady Harington at their house in Kew. Young Henry was interested in all things naval and military and also in history and the arts – but did not share his father's interest in the pursuit of animals. 'You are no sportsman' said the King. But in 1610 Prince Henry aged sixteen, was given his own household establishment and was invested as Prince of Wales. He gathered his own court around him at St James's and Richmond, and in September 1610 he was formally granted the Palace of Richmond as a residence and the manors of Richmond, Petersham and Ham. His mind turned at once to major works.

From the Grand Duke of Tuscany he obtained the services of Costantino de' Servi as a polymath court artist – architect – garden designer – sculptor – producer of masques – whatever. However de' Servi could not arrive until June 1611 and in the meantime Henry pressed ahead with the help of his official architect, the Frenchman

Solomon de Caux, and his young surveyor, Inigo Jones. It is clear that the intended works included three elements: some reclamation of the river bank by the palace, incorporating three small islands with bridges and 'stairs'; the filling in of of the old moat and the construction of a new canal and cistern house; and the erection of artificial mountains with giant figures and fountains, designed by de Caux, some of them perhaps intended to be on the islands, as these were to have water piped to them from the cistern house.

When de' Servi arrived he submitted a plan for some alterations to the southern front of the Privy Lodgings building – the addition of two flanking wings and a central loggia – and a complete redesign of the gardens, involving a very considerable reclamation of land from the river and a total remodelling of the layout between Crane Piece (now Old Palace Lane) and Water Lane (this is the plan discovered in Florence and published in 1998). There was evidently some ill feeling between de' Servi and Caux and Jones, but de' Servi claimed that his plans had been preferred both by the Prince and the King. But funds were not forthcoming.

In the summer of 1612 Prince Henry and de' Servi discussed a complete rebuilding of the palace in the latest Italian style, to be ready for the Prince's intended bride Maria of Savoy. But then de' Servi asked to be recalled to Florence; he had not been paid for a year. And in October the Prince contracted typhoid and died within a couple of weeks, on 6 November 1612.

All work was stopped, except some clearing up. Inigo Jones had already built the cistern house (which later became an armoury); the moat had almost certainly been filled; a base had been built for one of the intended artificial mountains close to Crane Wharf (the 'rockhouse', as it was called, was later turned into a brew-house); and Jones appears to have filled in the spaces between the islands to make a more or less straight river-line from Crane Wharf up to the wharf by Water Lane.

For four years Richmond Palace remained in the King's hands but when Prince Charles in his turn reached the age of 16 he was invested as Prince of Wales and was granted the palace and the three manors. Charles had no architectural ambitions for Richmond. He continued to build up the collection of pictures and sculptures which his brother had started, but about the only works carried out were the conversion of the cistern house into an armoury,

Charles, Prince of Wales

the demolition of a new tennis court which Henry had built somewhere in the grounds, the provision of a shuffleboard room (probably in the galleries) and the construction of a new pheasant house in the orchard.

Richmond Palace c.1630 (the 'Fitzwilliam painting')

When Charles became King he made over Richmond Palace with the manors of Richmond, Petersham and Ham to his new wife Henrietta Maria of France. The palace again became a base for the royal children, starting with the eldest, Prince Charles (the future Charles II), who was set up there at the age of four with his tutor the Reverend Brian Duppa. Duppa remained at Richmond as the Prince's tutor even when appointed Bishop of Chichester in 1638, until he became Bishop of Salisbury in 1641. In 1638 Prince Charles was given his own household establishment, but he was only eight and the palace and the manors remained in the hands of his mother. There were no major new works at the palace at this time; the important royal work at Richmond was the enclosure of Charles I's great New Park up on the hill.

Richmond Palace in 1638 by Hollar

The contest of wills between Charles and Parliament was coming to a crisis in 1640–41. Though Parliament had achieved a bloodless constitutional victory by the end of 1641 a series of blunders then plunged the country into civil war. In February 1641/2 the Queen and the young Princess Mary had been sent to the safety of the Netherlands. The Marquess of Hertford, newly appointed Governor to Prince

Charles, got his charge and the Duke of York away from Richmond to join the King at Greenwich, and then to go with him to Oxford.

The King never returned to Richmond Palace. When he became a prisoner of the parliamentary army in 1647, Parliament approved of his being allowed to take up residence there, and the palace was prepared to receive him. But the army, which was already at odds with Parliament, preferred to house him at Hampton Court, because it was a little further away from the capital.

THE PARLIAMENTARY SURVEY AND SALE

After Charles I's execution in 1649 and the formal abolition of the monarchy, Parliament set about raising money through the sale of most of the royal estates, amongst which was Richmond Palace. To this end a detailed survey of it (though unfortunately without a plan) was made in December 1649, and it confirms that the general layout had hardly changed in the century and a half since the description written in 1501. It gives us many useful extra details: for example some dimensions of the hall and chapel and the courts; a detailed description of the kitchen and other domestic offices; the precise number of trees in the orchards and gardens; an account of the main rooms within the Privy Lodgings (and of their use in 1649). There is also an account of the Little Park (King James's) and its hunting lodge, the ferry across the river, of Richmond Green and the Queen's Stables on the opposite side of the Green, and so on, a recital of the customs of the manor and a list of the rents paid by the manor tenants. The whole was valued. 'The materials of the said Manor House or Palace of Richmond and of the gardens orchards and offices belonging to the same are valued to be worth £10,782.19s.2d.' The site was valued at an extra £217.6s.8d. There were separate figures for the Little Park and its lodge, for the rents and so on.

The palace, together with the Green and the ferry, the Queen's Stables, some small pieces of land and the lordship of the manor, was sold on 10 July 1650 to a three- man consortium for the sum of £13,562.0s.6d. The purchasers then appear to have divided the property. The outlying pieces were sold off. The lordship of the manor and the brick buildings of the outer court and along the wall facing the Green were acquired by Sir Gregory Norton. Most of the rest – the stone buildings of the Middle Gate, Hall, Chapel and Privy Lodgings, together with the garden galleries, went to one Henry Carter. Norton and his heirs divided up their part of the palace and leased it out as separate dwellings. Carter seems to have treated his part simply as a stone quarry. As an informant reported in June 1660 'Henry Carter was the first puller-down of the King's house ... and sold the stone and material of the house to the value of £2,000 and upwards ... and was one of the good buyers himself ... and raised forces within these last three months to oppose the Restoration'.

Demolition must have started almost at once. In October of 1651 an inhabitant was fined by the manor court 'for driving his cart loaden with stones ... from the Great House cross Richmond Green out of the usual way'. By 1660 there was nothing left of the stone buildings except the Middle Gate.

chapter 5

The Palace site after 1660

Shortly after the restoration of King Charles II in May 1660, the Surveyor-General of Crown Lands was sent to inspect what remained of Richmond Palace. The parliamentary sales that had taken place were, as might be expected, declared invalid and the palace and manor had been formally restored to Queen Henrietta Maria. She, however, made no attempt to return to Richmond and soon leased the lordship of the manor to Sir Edward Villiers, who had meanwhile in July 1660 been appointed Keeper of the House and the [Little] Park and of the late [Charterhouse] Monastery of Shene and Steward of the manor and its courts. In 1664 the manor and the palace were granted to James Duke of York, in reversion after the death of the Queen. (She died in France in 1669.)

The Surveyor-General reported that the palace and its outbuildings had been divided up into 25 separate parcels, many of which were claimed by Henry Carter. Already some petitions had been received requesting new leases, especially for the most valuable remaining parts of the property. It was soon evident that the King had no desire to rebuild, so the granting of leases was left in the hands of Villiers, who was allowed to reside in that part of the palace in best repair – and still reserved in royal hands – the front range from the gate eastwards, plus the wardrobe. Villiers was the uncle of Charles II's mistress, Barbara Villiers, Countess of Castlemain; and his wife Lady Villiers was appointed governess to the Duke of York's daughters Mary and Anne – both future Queens. Richmond again became a royal nursery; but, despite its healthy reputation, two of the Duke's young sons died there.

NEW BUILDINGS ON THE SITE

The first new building to be erected on the site had in fact predated the Restoration. It was a house built by Henry Carter in the old open tennis court. This was the origin of the central block of 'Tudor Place' . Two wings were added to this building before 1725, and in the 1830s the whole range was redeveloped into the three houses that stand on the site today. (See illustration p.40)

After Carter's house on the tennis court site, there seems to have been no further building until some works of restoration were put in hand after the accession of James II (the former Duke of York) and the birth in 1688 of his son James Edward. These works were in the charge of Christopher Wren, but he had not got far when James was driven from the throne, and work was stopped. Detailed accounts for these works in 1688–89 survive, and are of interest for the names they give to all the rooms then occupied, but it is virtually impossible to sort these out into a plan. Although much of the work was decorative, there are several mentions of 'new. walls' and of a 'new building' which is almost certainly the link building between the back of the gatehouse and the wardrobe.

Trumpeters' House

In 1695 the then Steward of the Manor, Lord Capel, reported that 'several tenements are much out of repair and decayed and have for many years stood empty, some whereof need rebuilding, others cannot be put into any tenantable condition without the laying out of great sums of money'. It was not however until the first years of the 18th century that rebuilding really started. In 1700 the diplomat Richard Hill was granted a lease of the Middle Gate and the adjacent buildings, then used only to a house the gardener who looked after the gardens which now occupied the sites of the former Chapel, Fountain Court and the Privy Lodgings, also included in Hill's lease. A new house was built for him by John Yeomans in 1703–04 on the site of (and actually incorporating some of) the Middle Gate building. It was called Trumpeters' House as the two stone figures of trumpeters which had adorned the old gate were re-erected on the new house. (The two wings and the large portico on the river front were added in the mid-1740s.)

In 1705 a lease was granted to Alexander Cutting of the ruinous buildings on the west side of the main gate and he replaced them with two new houses, completed in 1708. These houses, now called 'Old Court House' and 'Wentworth House' were originally an identical pair, but the former acquired a new bow and entrance door in the late 18th century and the latter was largely rebuilt in the mid-19th century.

In 1708 General Sir George Cholmondeley (later Earl of Cholmondeley) who had become Steward of the Manor in 1702, was granted a 50-year lease of the royal apartments. His petition, the 'particulars' and the lease itself all made a point of the state of disrepair of the buildings. Obviously the works of 1688–89 had not included the rebuilding of the garden front of the Wardrobe, however 'Wren-ish' that may now appear. It seems certain that it was in the next year or two after 1708 that that work was carried out.

Maids of Honour Row

In 1724–25, some years after the new Prince of Wales (the future George II) and his wife Caroline had moved into the lodge in the Old Deer Park, it was found necessary to provide extra accommodation for the Princess's ladies-in-waiting or 'maids of honour' as they were then called. This was achieved by knocking down most of the old buildings facing the Green between the main gate and 'Tudor Place' and building in their place a row of new houses, to be called 'Maids of Honour Row'. As Caroline had six 'maids of honour' it is probable that only three houses were originally planned, but a fourth (No 1) was then squeezed in, between – and around – the western end of Tudor Place and the first of the new houses already under construction. The front facades look identical, but No 1 is much narrower at the back. Lord Cholmondeley continued to own the main lease of the houses until his death in 1733, but his son sold them in 1735.

In the late 1730s the new Earl of Cholmondeley began to build by the river. His father had acquired from Richard Hill in 1711 a part of the garden behind the site of the former Chapel, including a broad strip of land which enabled him to make a walk about 45 feet wide down from his property by the Green to the riverside. A new lease granted to him in 1730 included also a lot more of the original Privy Gardens of the palace, of the remains of the galleries (which had had some small houses converted out of, or tacked onto, them) and part of the land between these and the river. Because one of the houses built onto the galleries had been called, misleadingly, the 'Friars', this land which was part of that reclaimed in 1611–12, had also been called 'the Friars Ground'.

About 1738 Lord Cholmondeley built, at the southern end of this land, a new library – a building shaped like a long cross with rounded ends and protruding central bays, one of which encroached on the previously untenanted riverside walk on the Friars' Ground. This encroachment was dealt with by granting the whole Friars' Ground to Cholmondeley, so long as a right of way for pedestrians was maintained by the riverside. He then built a new mansion by the river called Cholmondeley House, completed about 1748 and joined onto the eastern end of the library.

At about the same time Cholmondeley pulled down the long north-south range of building that stood between the main gate and the new Maids of Honour Row, together with an adjacent part of the old front wall, and put up a new east end to the gatehouse building, with a wide bay to match the original one by the gate. The result was a pastiche, more less symmetrical, with one Tudor bay and one 18th century one, and a smaller 'tower' in between them which is part Tudor and part later – the whole being now the dwellings called 'Old Palace' and 'Palace Gate House'. When his new riverside mansion was ready, he sold off this building and the Wardrobe.

'Old Palace' (then including the gatehouse) and the Wardrobe were divided by the new owner into separate residences. There was little more work done on the Wardrobe until a medical tenant in the mid-19th century added a small building at the southern end of the front to house a consulting room, surgery and waiting room. The building was divided into three separate residences by the Crown Estate Commissioners in 1956.

'Old Palace' benefited – or suffered – from several 'restorations'. In the mid-18th century stucco had been applied to the walls and 'Queen Anne' windows had been inserted, together with a most obtrusive oriel window above the actual gate arch. In the 1880s the stucco and the 'Queen Anne' windows were removed, the top of the central bay and some parapets and chimneys were rebuilt. An enthusiastic, but muddle-headed, antiquarian occupied the building from 1907 and spent much money on further 'restoration', changing the windows once again. His offers to give the house to the nation as a 'Tudor museum' or as a chapter house for the Order of the British Empire were met by the reminder that it was crown property and that he would first have to buy it – at a considerable price. The schemes were abandoned. When the lease finally fell in in 1938 the Crown Estate Commissioners decided to divide the house into two separate dwellings. The archway was restored and the oriel window above it removed. In 1976 the arms of Henry VII were restored.

Asgill House

The other main new building in the palace area was not in fact on ground which had been part of the Tudor palace but was where Inigo Jones had started to build the 'rock house' by the river adjacent to Crane Wharf. It probably stood right over the end of the old moat. This had become a brewhouse in the late 17th century. In 1756 this and the land behind it up to the side passage into the palace were acquired by the Jewish merchant and financier Moses Hart. He also bought and demolished the 'six ruinous tenements' on the south side of that passage – the remains of dwellings made out of some of the kitchen quarters – and a strip of the old orchard, which widened his ground to a frontage, by the river, of over 170 feet. He applied for a new lease, but then died; and his heirs sold the property to Sir Charles Asgill, Lord Mayor of London in 1757–58. Asgill got his friend Sir Robert Taylor, the architect, to build him an elegant riverside villa. It was finished by the time his new lease was granted in 1762. Asgill House was much enlarged about 1840 by its then tenant, and its appearance was altered by building up the two wings to the height of the central block. The house was restored to its original size and plan in 1967–70.

In 1780 Cholmondeley House was purchased by the Duke of Queensberry, 'old Q'. It had been further enlarged after the houses in Cholmondeley Walk had been built in the 1760s and Friars' Lane, originally straight, had been diverted round them. The ground taken out of the southern end of the lane was added to Cholmondeley House and a new carriage entrance made there. 'Old Q' was one of Richmond's outstanding characters: a dandy and a wit, with a passion for gambling, horse racing, music and the fair sex, he entertained lavishly and gave generously to charity. But he quarrelled with the local people when he tried to enclose the riverside walk and left Richmond in disgust in 1801. In 1828 Queensberry House (as it was then called), in a bad state of disrepair, was acquired by Sir William Dundas.

Two years later Dundas was able to secure the freehold in a deal by which he gave up land elsewhere to be added to the royal farm. He then pulled down the old building and built a new mansion, Queensberry Villa, further back from the river, laying out gardens between the house and the riverside walk. This in its turn was replaced by the Queensberry House flats in 1934. (It may be noted that the brick tower building at the bend in Friars' Lane is nothing to do with the Tudor palace. It was put up by Dundas in the 1830s to house a water pump.)

A number of buildings along Friars' Lane which were made out of, or built upon part of, the former galleries, have all been demolished. The house called 'The Friars' disappeared between 1739 and 1756 and one next to it between 1771 and 1783. Both of these were on land which was granted to the Earl of Cholmondeley in 1730. About mid-way down the lane a group of four small cottages stood close together in 1660. These were gradually rebuilt in the mid-18th century into one quite large house, which was sold to the Duke of Queensberry in the 1780s. It was demolished in the early 19th century and its site used as stables until replaced by Hunters Court in 1961. In the 19th century there were other stables behind the Tudor Place-Tudor Lodge houses. These also were on the site of the garden galleries. They were replaced by Elyston Mews in 1983.

There are other 20th century buildings on the palace site. The row of four small houses called 1–4 Old Palace Yard, on its western side, replaced stables and work-shops in 1950. Trumpeters' Inn, on the site of one-time kitchen premises and later stables and workshops on the south side of the side entrance to Old Palace Yard, was built in 1956, shortly after Trumpeters' House was converted into four flats and a small house (Trumpeters' Lodge). By the end of this side lane, where it emerges into Old Palace Lane, is a group of four houses (Nos 27–30) built in 1972–73. Their site is that of the one-time cistern house or armoury and of the north-west corner of the moat. (Asgill Lodge in Old Palace Lane was built in 1756 on land which was origi-nally part of Crane Piece, outside the wall of the Clerk of Works' yard.)

Facing the corner of the Green, next to Wentworth House, at the north-west cor-ner of the palace site, a house was built in the 1880s after the demolition of the 18th century theatre which had stood – outside the palace site – at the corner of Old Palace Lane. This was called, in allusion to the theatre, Garrick House. It was replaced in 1962 by the development of six small houses named Garrick Close.

The site of the Friary (the former Byfleet) was leased out as gardens. A smaller section went to the house now called 'Old Friars' (which does not itself stand on the Friary site), while the greater part was leased to successive occupants of the houses which became 'Old Palace Place'. In the 1650s a house was built in this larger section, by the eastern boundary, backing onto the cottages in Water Lane. By the end of the 17th century the path between the Friary and the palace had been widened and straightened, and the empty ground between the river and the Friary site had been added to the leased ground. In the early 18th century some development started: a malthouse towards the southern end of the east side, followed by a precursor of the White Cross tavern (almost certainly called the Waterman's Arms) about 1728. Some stabling for Cholmondeley House was built in 1757, then the houses called Cholmondeley Lodge and Cholmondeley Villa (and the diversion of Friars' Lane) in the late 1760s, followed by a row of cottages called White Cross Buildings (since demolished) parallel to Water Lane in the 1770s and a row of boathouses in the 1790s. The freeholds of the whole site were sold off in lots in 1833. The northern end remained gardens, but St Helena Terrace was built where the boathouses had been, and a brewery took the place of the Cholmondeley House stables (now the open car park). Queensberry Villas were built in Friars' Lane. A new private road was opened up from Friars' Lane, with Villa Retreat at its far end and later with Retreat Villas on its south side. A group of modern houses now fills the garden of Villa Retreat.

PART TWO

RECOVERING THE PLAN OF THE TUDOR PALACE

chapter 6

A review of the sources

SURVIVING BUILDINGS

Obviously any surviving parts of the Tudor palace provide irrefutable evidence of the part they occupied in the plan. But problems remain. It is not always quite clear where the Tudor work begins and ends. Even such certain relics as the gatehouse and gateway and the wardrobe have been altered and repaired very many times.

ARCHAEOLOGICAL FINDS

A few finds were noted, but not well recorded, up to the middle of the 20th century. Since then there have been a few 'rescue archaeology' observations on sites being redeveloped, a three-day dig in the Trumpeters' House lawn by the Channel 4 'Time Team' programme, and some pioneer work by the Richmond Archaeological Society along the riverbank. There has however been no serious archaeological survey of the site as a whole.

Painted glass from Richmond Palace

DESCRIPTIONS

There are two principal contemporary verbal descriptions of the palace: one, just after its building, is the herald's account in 1501 (see above p.11); the other, just before its destruction, is the survey carried out by order of Parliament before the building was sold in 1650. To these a few extra details can be added from briefer accounts of the palace by visitors (often foreign) in the century and a half of its heyday.

PICTURES

Most important are the sketches made by the Flemish artist Antonis van Wyngaerde when he visited Richmond in 1561–62 and now held by the Ashmolean Museum,

Oxford. There are five preliminary sketches and two finished drawings of the palace, seen from the Green and from across the river. The former sketches, obviously done on the spot, are more detailed and often clearer than the finished drawings, which were worked up later.

Two important depictions date from the 1620's and 1630's. (see p.26) One, a large oil painting by an unidentified Flemish artist in the Fitzwilliam Museum, Cambridge, shows the palace and the Richmond riverside as seen from the Twickenham bank a little way above the ferry place (now the site of Richmond Bridge). The other is an engraving by Wenceslaus Hollar dated 1638. It appears to have been the inspiration for a number of very similar oil paintings produced at about the same time, the best known of which belongs to the Society of Antiquaries of London. Hollar made another drawing depicting the view from Richmond Hill down towards the palace which is distant and not shown in great detail.

Richmond Palace: The Society of Antiquaries' painting (based on Hollar?)

Other contemporary versions, such as the illustration in a corner of Speed's map of Surrey or the somewhat impressionistic rendering in Moses Glovers's map of Isleworth Hundred (at Syon House) are far less detailed and less accurate.

There are a few later drawings and engravings which are useful in recording the progress of demolition and rebuilding on the palace site. A small drawing of the palace front facing the Green (see pp.40–41), by F Gasselin about 1695 (in the Museum of Richmond), can be compared with Wyngaerde's sketch of nearly a century and a half earlier. The 'Prospect of Richmond Surry' [sic], published in 1726, and the engraving of a drawing by Shaftoe (see p.42), published in Groves' *Life of Wolsey* in 1742, show considerable redevelopment in addition to some features of the Tudor palace then still surviving but now disappeared. And there are, of course, several depictions of the 18th century Cholmondeley and Asgill Houses.

PLANS

There are only two known plans of any parts of the palace made before its mid-17th century destruction. The recent discovery (published in *Apollo* magazine, November 1998) in the Medici archives in Florence of a plan apparently drawn up in 1611 by Costantino de' Servi has produced a carefully drawn outline of the Privy Lodgings building, with a scale in English feet. While this shows the alterations which de' Servi planned for the south facade of the building, the other three facades are apparently unaltered (and tie in well with the existing illustrations). The plan also shows the bridge over the moat from the Privy Lodgings to the Fountain Court and, in an adjacent rectangle, an indication of the Fountain Court buildings. De' Servi's new layout for the gardens required a lot of reclamation work from the river and can only be linked to the actual layout on the ground (then or now) at Crane Wharf and at Water Lane.

A very rough 'back of an envelope' plan by Inigo Jones (in the Public Record Office) was probably made in 1612 and shows, with a very approximate outline of the

de' Servi's Plan

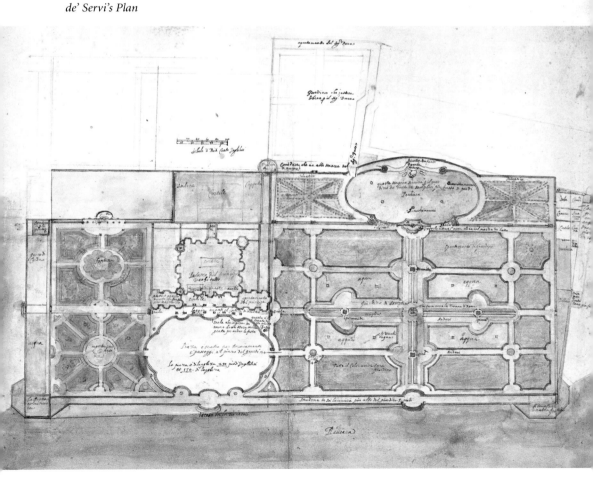

south side of the palace, some of the work done by Jones on the riverbank: the new cistern house, pipes or channels connecting this with a structure by the riverside, the crane, and some lines indicating proposed (and accomplished?) reclamation.

There are also some later plans, which are of much value for the history of the site and of some value for considering the Tudor plan. These are:

- A plan of c1701 (PRO MPE 428) shows boundaries within the now divided-up site rather than actual buildings.

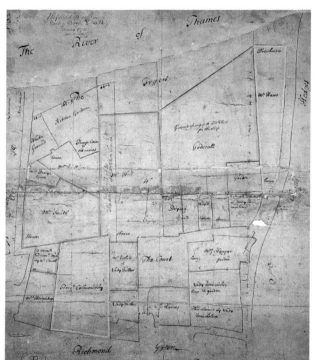

Plan of Richmond Palace, 1701

- John Rocque's map of 'The Country Ten Miles Round London' (1745) gives a fair, but only approximate and small scale, indication of the buildings then on the site. (Trumpeters' House is omitted because it was then undergoing alterations.)
- A detailed and accurate, large scale (25 yards: 2 inches) survey of the whole palace site in 1756 (PRO MPE 362).
- The detailed plan (at a scale of 3 chains: 2 inches, or roughly 100 feet to an inch) accompanying the Manor Survey of 1771 (PRO CRES 5/347 plan A) shows little change from that of 1756, save in Asgill House.
- Ordnance Survey maps at a scale of 25 inches to a mile or 1:2500 from 1863 onwards.

Plans accompanying lease documents do not as a rule add much to the reconstruction of the palace plan. Only a few predate the 1756 plan and there are several based on that plan. A few later plans, useful mainly for the history of the individual houses, are of Tudor Place 1781, Queensberry House 1782, the garden behind Old Friars 1801, Old Palace 1801, Old Court House 1808 and Asgill House 1810.

LEASE DOCUMENTS

The documents dealing with crown leases on the various properties within the site after the 1680s (which are preserved in the PRO) often give very useful information, especially dimensions, which help to deduce the size and exact location of buildings that have subsequently disappeared. The normal procedure was for the would-be tenant to present a petition requesting a lease. This was referred to the Surveyor General, who would submit a detailed report on the property - 'the particulars' - to the Treasury. If the lease was agreed, the Treasury would issue a warrant and the actual lease would then be drawn up. The 'particulars' sometimes gave details on the past history of the property which enables it to be tied in exactly to the 1650 survey.

WORKS ACCOUNTS, ETC

Although there are unfortunately no extant accounts giving details of the major rebuilding work in 1497–1501, accounts do survive for many of the minor works carried out between then and 1650. There are also detailed accounts for the works of repair and redecoration carried out for James II under the supervision of Sir Christopher Wren in 1688–89. These again shed useful light on the history of the palace, but not much on its plan.

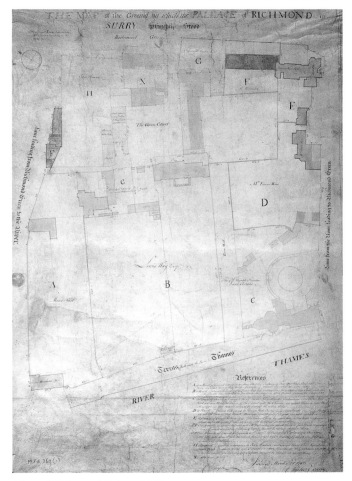

Plan of Richmond Palace, 1756

chapter 7

The Pre-Tudor layout

As mentioned above (see p.5) the original manor house and Edward III's palace had two courts: a 'down court' by the river and an 'over court' between the down court and the Green. These two courts were separated by the moat, which is referred to as early as 1361–62. In 1371 the moat was cleaned – a length of 874 feet 6 inches. When it was cleaned again in 1376 only 738 feet were done.

Documents referring to the works on the Lancastrian palace clearly distinguish between three adjacent sites: 'the old manor of Shene', 'the new manor of Shene' and the 'the manor of Byfleet at Shene'. In 1414 a ditch was dug 'between the manor of Shene and the new timber building called Byfleet'. In 1436–39 a new moat 25 feet wide and eight feet deep was dug between 'the old site of the manor of Shene' and 'the new building of the manor of Shene'. As Byfleet was certainly on the site of the later Friary, we can now say that 'the old manor of Shene' was at the western end of the complex, the 'new manor' and its gardens in the centre, and 'Byfleet' at the eastern end.

Wyngaerde's drawings show the eastern arm of the moat between the Privy Lodgings and the privy gardens. While the northern arm is not clearly depicted, there are indications: overflow pipes from the water cisterns presumably discharge into it, as would the culvert arches from the house of office. That the moat lay between the Privy Lodgings and the Fountain Court is confirmed by the bridge shown in de' Servi's plan. The western arm of the moat is not clearly drawn by Wyngaerde, but a great wide V in the riverbank shown in Hollar's engraving presumably marks its former site.

If we then measure the moat as it must have been in Tudor times we have a distance of some 900 feet for the three arms together and 750 feet if the eastern arm is omitted. Considering that the river bank may have been advanced some 12 feet since the 1370's the fit with the dimensions quoted above is almost exact. Why should the eastern arm have been omitted from the 1376 cleansing operation? The answer must be that the building works of the 1370s hardly affected that side of the moat, which bordered the palace gardens rather than the buildings.

Archaeological evidence exists for the line of the northern arm of the moat – a wall uncovered during the building works at 27–30 Old Palace Lane in 1972, and finds (wrongly attributed at the time) during the Time Team excavation in 1997.

It seems possible that the original northern wall of the manor house and the early palaces was on a line with that of 'Byfleet'. 'Byfleet' was probably erected in what had been the small park attached to the manor house (mentioned in 1292), and it is likely that the new garden of the Lancastrian palace was also carved out of this park. Then in 1445 came the instructions to the Clerk of Works to 'new make a great quadrangle with a gatehouse all of new' and 'a new brick wall to enclose the garden'. This must mark a decision to enlarge the palace by encroaching on the Green. A few years later the site of what are now Old Palace Terrace and Paved Court was granted to the Charterhouse, and it seems probable that land between this and the north wall of the Friary was granted out for building (the present south side of King Street) at about this same time.

Approximate diagrams of the layout of the 14th and 15th century palaces are shown here. The conclusions are that the original manor house and Edward III's palace stood in what is now in part the grounds of Asgill House and in part the garden of Trumpeters' Lodge, and that the Lancastrian palace by the time it was completed had almost exactly the same layout as the Tudor palace.

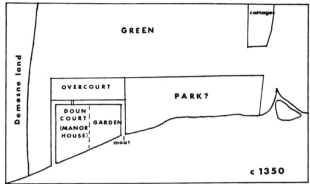

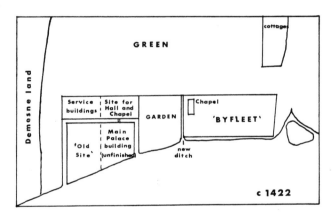

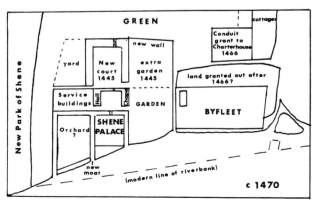

The site of the 14th and 15th century Palaces (not to scale)

chapter 8

The plan of the Tudor Palace

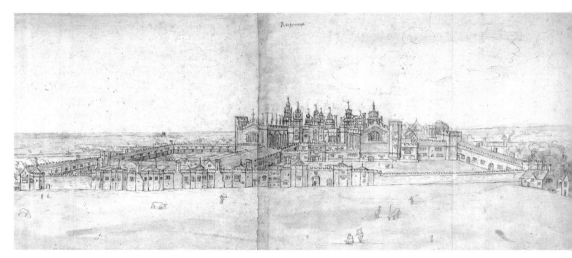

Richmond Palace from the Green by Wyngaerde

THE GATE, GATEHOUSE AND BUILDINGS ON THE FRONT TO THE EAST SIDE OF THE GATE

The basic structure of the gateway and the gatehouse on its east side are surviving relics of the Tudor palace. We can therefore follow the plan of these buildings as far as the central tower on the Green side of the present 'Old Palace' and as far as the staircase tower behind the gatehouse. As explained in Chapter 5, the east end of 'Old Palace' and the link building between the gatehouse and the Wardrobe are later additions. The Wyngaerde drawing and the drawing of c.1690 by F. Gasselin show the original appearance of the outer wall of the palace in this area, and the 'Prospect of Richmond' and the Shaftoe engraving (see p.42) show the north-south range which stood at the east of the buildings set back by the gate.

From the Parliamentary Survey of 1649 we know that there was another gate leading into the Wine Cellar Court, and we can see this gate in Wyngaerde's drawing, a little to the east (left) of the 'Old Palace' central tower. We have no exact dimensions for the Wine Cellar Court, but it presumably stretched down behind the Wardrobe

to the wine cellars which we know from the 1649 survey to have been under the Chapel.

In 1660 Walter Long, who had rented these buildings from Sir Henry Norton, applied for a new lease. In his report the Surveyor General listed one building 32 feet broad and 60 feet long (the Gatehouse), one building 'abutting on the Green' 72 feet in length and 20 feet broad (the north-south range) and another building called the Prince's Lodgings 164 feet in length and 22 feet in breadth, with a piece of ground enclosed by a brick wall 164 feet by 40 feet and a yard 164 feet by 14 feet. (PRO CRES 6/2 p.75)

This latter building can be neatly fitted into the space between the north-south range and the tennis court. It is uncertain exactly where the north and south walls of the north-south range and of the long east-west range should be. The pictures mentioned above give us an approximate position: the north end of the north-south range was nearly level with the front of Maids of Honour Row, the east-west range was set back a little. If we postulate that its southern wall was where the southern wall of Maids of Honour Row now stands, the 40 foot ground fits in neatly on the north (Green) side and the 14 foot yard on the internal side.

A substantial east-west wall of 16th century brick was found in 1991 just to the south of the present south wall of the 18th century part of Old Palace. This may well be the southern end of the north-south range.

The Wyngaerde drawing shows us where the open tennis court stood, behind a blank section of outer wall, and shows the end of the galleries, where the banqueting house was situated, on its eastern side. The drawing of the gardens (see p.48) shows how the galleries also turned round to the west behind the tennis court, ending in a small staircase tower. That tower (or at least its lower part) survives today. It was originally attached to the western wing of the new house built in the tennis court, then transferred to 1 Maids of Honour Row. It gives us a fixed point for the end of the galleries here and for the south wall of the tennis court. The plan of 1756 shows the house in the tennis court and the canted shape of this tower, as also what is unmistakably the line of the easternmost tower in the front wall, and the adjacent banqueting house as seen in the Wyngaerde and Gasselin drawings. These drawings enable us to insert details such as the towers and chimneys on the front wall by the Green.

THE WARDROBE

The Wardrobe was also the subject of a lease petition in 1660. Robert Roane who had been Under-Keeper of the palace, and who was noted in the 1649 survey as

Drawing of the front of the Palace facing the Green by Gasselin, c.1695

Richmond Palace in 1742 by W. Shaftoe

having 'some years ago' saved the palace at risk of his own life when a fire started in the Wardrobe rooms, had bought the Wardrobe building in 1652. The Surveyor General noted that the building – part brick and part timber – was 120 feet long by 28 feet broad (PRO CRES 6/3). This shows that in 1660 it was free standing and not connected with the Gatehouse. Its western wall facing Old Palace Yard is basically Tudor, though the windows are later, and the big arches (probably to allow for the loading and unloading of carts under cover) have been filled in. (The eastern wall, as noted above, dates from c1710 and the link building to the Gatehouse is probably 1688–89.) The Surveyor General's report also gave the dimensions of three separate plots of garden attached to the Wardrobe. These can be fitted in behind the Wardrobe and possibly were all parts of the Wine Cellar Court.

OLD COURT HOUSE AND WENTWORTH HOUSE

The 1701 plan shows the 'ruins' on the west side of the gate, with a rough indication of another protruding north-south range. This can be seen in the Wyngaerde drawing, and with greater clarity in the Gasselin one. There is evidently a block of two-storey buildings near the gate, then a long section of blank wall (which would have had single-storey apartments or offices on the inside) terminating in a corner tower. The 1756 plan shows two new houses (now Old Court House and Wentworth House) and the same corner tower, though the wall extends beyond the latter up to Old Palace Lane, (the extra, western, court outside the main palace buildings having been the Clerk of Works' yard). The particulars (PRO E376/3817) of the lease granted in 1705 to Alexander Cutting, who built the houses, gives us the exact dimensions of the plot of ground being leased but not, unfortunately, of the then existing buildings within it. However there is a plan with a dotted line that shows the shape of the eastern and northern walls. The position of the southern wall is conjectured.

THE NORTH-WEST CORNER AND WEST RANGE
OF THE GREAT COURT

Although there is plenty of documentation concerning the lease of the corner property to the Countess of Winchelsea in 1700 (and the lease held by her father John Ayres from 1669) there are no dimensions given. The part of the old palace covered by the Countess's lease was largely already demolished, and it is defined by reference to the abutting properties.

To the south of this property however was one that had been in the occupation of Symon Hopper since the 1650s and on which a new lease was granted to his widow Ann in 1705 (PRO E367/3812). The area leased included a yard which was taken out of the Great Court, a range of buildings on the west side of the court, and a garden, stable and yards outside these, up to Old Palace Lane (which had been part of the Clerk of Works' yard). The dimensions of the plot are given, and an accompanying plan shows the detailed outline of 'Mrs Hopper's house'. This is evidently part of the old western range of the Great Court, though it would appear that various outbuildings had probably been built up on the western side. The plan shows the position of the 'old plummery' and the 'old gateway' leading into the side lane out to Old Palace Lane.

We can extend the lines of 'Mrs Hopper's house' up to the corner tower in the Countess of Winchelsea's property to give us the probable lines of the entire western range.

THE MIDDLE GATE AND FOUNTAIN COURT INCLUDING
GREAT HALL AND CHAPEL

The Wyngaerde drawing of the Great Court (see p.11) shows the Middle Gate with its archway and oriel window – and at least one of the two trumpeter figures adorning the thin turrets which framed it. It stood over to the east side of the Court – approximately where the entrance to Trumpeters' House stands today. The lease to Richard Hill in 1700 refers to it as 'the Garden Gate House or Trumpeting House' and the surveyor's report confirms that it stood 'opposite the gateway next Richmond Green' (PRO CRES 6/21, p.187). Next to the gate in the Wyngaerde picture is a short section of wall with a large oriel on the left (east) and a longer wall on the right (west) joining up with the front wall of the Great Hall – on exactly the same line. It seems certain that the northern facade of Trumpeters' House follows the line of these Tudor buildings – even including the fact that the wall on the eastern side of the door is set back some four feet further than that on the west. The 1649 survey gave a length of 100 feet for the Hall; only 96 feet for the Chapel (these are probably internal dimensions, but they match this four feet difference).

When Trumpeters' House was being converted into flats in 1951–52 some Tudor features incorporated into its fabric were revealed. Unfortunately these do not seem to have been properly recorded. The best account is given in Kathleen Courlander's *Richmond*. There was 'a perpendicular stone arch facing Henry VII's archway – the original entrance to the Middle Court. This was broken up and taken away. Then three smaller arches and a stone wall … carved foliage appeared in the spandrels. [Now] … they are hidden behind pine-panelled hall walls.' This does tend to confirm that the central hall of Trumpeters' House represents the archway of the old gate. What the depth of the Tudor building was we can only speculate, but the 1649 survey tells us that the Fountain Court was 67 feet by 66 feet.

The Hill lease also covered a 'piece of void ground or yard belonging and next adjoining on the east to Trumpeting House, containing 42 feet in the front, 100 feet in depth.' Here was the site of the Chapel (internal dimensions 96 feet by 30 feet) and of the Prince's closet adjoining it (the low building seen on the left of Fountain Court in the Wyngaerde drawing). This ground was incorporated into the site of Trumpeters' House and its east wing. On the west side of Trumpeters' House the site of the Great Hall (internal dimensions 100 feet by 40 feet) can be seen in the 1756 plan as a 'yard' 49 feet across its northern end and 106 feet 8 inches in length. At the far, southern, end of Fountain Court was a gallery between the Hall and the Chapel which was stated by the 1649 survey to be 27 yards (81 feet) in length.

De' Servi's plan (see p.35) shows a single rectangle to represent Fountain Court and the buildings in it (with 'Hall', 'Court', and 'Chapel' inserted roughly in pencil in the appropriate places, as if added while the plan was being explained to Prince Henry or King James.) Taking dimensions from de' Servi's scale in feet, the rectangle would measure approximately 183 feet by 110 feet. A similar east-west measurement on the 1756 plan gives 183 feet from the west side of the empty yard to the east end of the Trumpeters' House wing – which suggests that de' Servi's plan in this part is accurate as to overall size however diagrammatic as to detail.

THE PRIVY LODGINGS BUILDING

From the gallery on the south side of Fountain Court, a bridge crossed the moat to give access to the Privy Lodgings. Although the moat had no part to play in de' Servi's plan for the new palace gardens, the bridge remained, and is clearly shown and marked as such ('*ponte*') on his plan. Its dimensions, as read from the plan, were some 30 feet in length by 20 feet in breadth, and it led straight into the canted bay in the centre of the north facade of the Privy Lodgings block.

De' Servi's intended alterations to this building were confined to the south side. New wing buildings were to be added extending from the corners. They were to be built in a style similar to that of the old building ('*da farsi simile al vechio*'). At the south-east corner the new wing would replace the watergate building seen in Wyngaerde's drawing. At the south-west corner the existing staircase tower (circular but with protruding ribs) would be retained. Between the wings would be a court-yard with a loggia, but only a part of the former south front was to be rebuilt to make a closer match with the rest (the plan shows the eastern part of the south front, including the central feature as '*questo e vechio*' (this is old) and the western part up to (but not including) the corner tower as '*nuovo*' (new).

The whole building is marked by de' Servi '*Palazzo del principe – vechi tutto*' (the Prince's palace – all old), and the bays and towers which he shows indeed fit very well with those seen in Wyngaerde's and Hollar's depictions and in the Fitzwilliam picture. We can therefore trust de' Servi's plan for this building. Measuring from his scale, the dimensions are: north to south (from the edge of the entrance bay to the southernmost part of the centre feature on the south face) 122 feet; east to west (from the outside of the central towers on each face) 140 feet. (The great canted tower at the north-east corner is in line on its north side with the entrance bay, but extends about five feet further to the east than the centre tower on the east side.) As shown on the plan, the western side of this rectangle is approximately level with the western side of the Great Hall; the eastern side is only just to the east of the western side of the Chapel.

This means that the whole building was somewhat smaller than had previously been believed, its longer axis (and also that of its central court which measured 40 feet by 24 feet), was east-west rather than north-south, and the whole was sited somewhat farther to the west than had appeared likely from the later boundaries shown in the 1701 and 1756 plans (roughly the present boundary between Trumpeters' House lawn and the Trumpeters' Lodge garden). It also explains why the Time Team dig failed to find the outer walls of the Privy Lodgings building. On the south and west sides I had pointed them to the wrong place; on the north side a strong line shown by geophysical survey was in fact the northern side of the moat and not, as they thought at the time, the site of the north wall of the Privy Lodgings.

The southernmost trench dug by the Time Team did however reveal a curious feature: a wall, just under two feet in width, of 15th or 16th century bricks, the base of which had not been found even after excavating to a depth of almost nine feet. It was abutted by an internal wall on the north side. This appears now, from the de' Servi plan, to be much too far south to have been part of the Privy Lodgings block – unless it marked the south end of a cellar extending underground from that building towards the river.

THE MOAT

Most of the evidence for the location of the moat has been considered above (see chapter 7). The rescue excavations on the site of the new houses at 27–30 Old Palace

Lane in 1972 revealed traces of a moat wall exactly on the line there suggested. Although these were at the time judged to be of early 17th century construction, it does seem probable that the moat was filled in at the time of Prince Henry's works in 1610–12. Both of the more northerly Time Team trenches uncovered traces on the north side of the moat.

We have only one ancient piece of information on the width and depth of moats at Richmond and that refers to a section of moat dug in 1436–39 between the old site and the new site of the palace, which was probably filled in again during Henry VII's rebuilding, if not sooner. It was 25 feet wide and 8 feet deep (PRO E01/479/7). However a width of 25 feet would fit very well also for the main moat, as the bridge over it was shown by de' Servi as some 30 feet in length.

THE KITCHEN QUARTERS

In this area, which lay to the north of the moat and to the west of the Great Hall, we have three sources to guide us as to the plan: the Wyngaerde drawing of 1561, the Parliamentary Survey almost a century later, in 1649, and the particulars for a lease granted in 1661. The survey is full of descriptive detail, but with no dimensions. But the particulars for the lease (CTB vol 7, p.1583) give us precise dimensions and identifications for two buildings and two yards within this area: 'a tenement of two storeys, part brick and part timber, 64 feet long by 17 feet wide, late the flesh larder and other offices adjoining ... with a little yard 18 feet by 16 feet'; and 'another tenement adjacent, part brick part timber, adjoining to the last westward, 52 feet by 26 feet, late part of the pastry and other offices there, with a yard or garden plot northwards 74 feet by 42 feet walled in.'

A careful comparison of these details with the 1649 survey and the Wyngaerde drawing enables us to make an almost certain identification of these buildings in the drawing. The 'house of office' also reveals itself with its pair of stepped gables and its

The kitchens and domestic offices by Wyngaerde

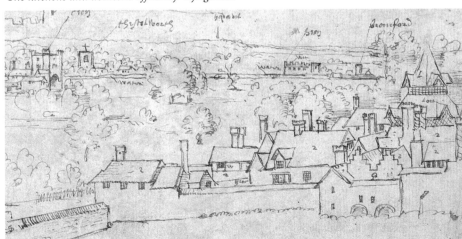

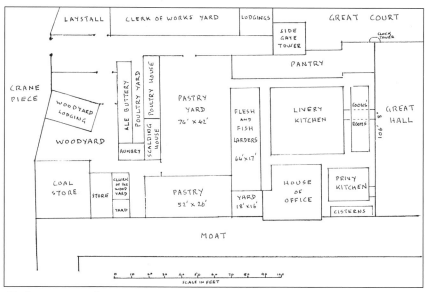

Kitchen quarters plan

two culverts where waste would be discharged into the moat. (One hopes the river, being tidal, would wash into and out of the moat and help to carry this waste away!) So does the great livery kitchen with its pyramidal louvred roof. It is interesting to note that, although a new livery kitchen was built in 1574–75, the depiction of the building in the Hollar engraving of 1638 shows very much the same design as that shown in the Wyngaerde drawing.

The location of the water cisterns is revealed by their overflow pipe discharging through the wall into the moat, and as the survey tells us that these were 'on the backside of the privy kitchen' that building can also be identified.

Not easily identifiable in the drawing of the kitchens, but clearly shown in that of the Great Court, and with its location pretty well fixed by the description in the survey, was the Pantry building, between the range 'which stands on the west side of the said Great Court and the said hall building'. It clearly had a step back in its front wall towards the Great Court, and this can be seen in the later plans.

Over on the left of the group of buildings seen in the Wyngaerde sketch of the kitchens is one with a three-stepped roof – the coal store, wood store and clerk of the woodyard's office – and then a half-timbered building farther from the moat wall which has to be the woodyard lodging.

Putting these indications together I believe that the domestic offices of the Tudor palace were as shown in the plan above.

THE GREAT ORCHARD

This, which is clearly seen in Wyngaerde's view of the palace from the river (see p.20), was the site of the early manor house and of Edward III's palace. Its outer wall towards the river still stands, for much of its length, between the main Trumpeters'

Lodge garden and the ground called 'Sarah's garden'. The high Tudor wall, running back obliquely, can be seen above the present outer wall from the riverside path.

In 1649 the Great Orchard was divided into a pattern of four square plots divided by alleys (but with a round space at their centre) and a large triangular plot. There were 223 fruit trees planted in these plots and a further 170 around the walls.

The eastward end of this wall was a good deal closer to the river than the south-west corner of the Privy Lodgings. A wall ran back from south to north to complete the enclosure of the orchard, with a gate in it onto the 'foreshore' of the palace (which can, incidentally, be seen through the window in the portrait of Prince Henry on p.24) The western wall of the orchard was of course by the moat.

In 1756 a strip of the orchard, about 85 feet wide, at its western side was sold by the Earl of Cholmondeley to Moses Hart, together with the old buildings at the northern end (which themselves represented successors to the original domestic buildings). We can therefore place the original western wall of the Tudor orchard this distance inside what are now the grounds of Asgill House.

THE PRIVY GARDENS AND THE GARDEN GALLERIES

We can see these in the Wyngaerde sketch. At the far end of the galleries is the tower, already mentioned, now attached to 1 Maids of Honour Row. At its right is a straight east-west section of gallery, being the part behind the tennis court. From there what appears to be another straight section (but which actually had a small dog-leg in it) leads down to the tower which is linked to the old (and by 1561 partly ruinous) chapel of the Friary by what must be a covered bridge over the footpath. From this tower an east-west wall runs back towards the main palace buildings. This is the lower part of the wall which today separates Queensberry House from the garden of the Wardrobe. By 1649 the part of the gardens to its north was called the Privy Garden and the part to the south the Privy Orchard. In former times both sections were the Privy Gardens.

Privy Gardens by Wyngaerde

From the central tower the galleries continued south for a bit, then bent round in a series of obtuse angled turns until they came to the moat on the east side of the Privy Lodgings. In 1517 a bridge was built to connect the galleries directly with the royal apartments. (From Wyngaerde's completed drawing of the palace from the river (see pp.20-21) there appears to be also another bridge over the moat, leading from the watergate building onto the open 'Friars' ground' outside the galleries.)

The 1649 survey says that the galleries were 200 yards in length, but does not make it clear exactly where the end points of this measurement come. De' Servi's plan sketches in lightly what are obviously intended to represent the northern part of the galleries, and shows the dog-leg clearly, but at this point he was no longer concerned with proposed alterations, and he does not seem to have troubled to survey the galleries accurately.

Though there are mentions in 17th century documents of the houses built onto, or out of, the galleries, it is in the 1756 plan (either the general one, or one of the same date accompanying a lease of the Cholmondeley House property to Earl Brooke) that we see enough of these old buildings to give a fairly accurate line for a large part of the south-east sections of the galleries. Farther to the north the house of Mrs Eleanor Wood (which replaced four of the cottages existing in 1660) has a significant canted corner opposite the part shown on this plan of the wall in the centre of the gardens. This might be the remains of the tower by the Friars's chapel.

It is easy to bring the line we have already established for the south-east part of the galleries round in one more obtuse-angled turn to meet up with this 'tower'. Further north again the 1756 plan shows a dog-leg in the boundary wall against Friars' Lane which corresponds well enough with the one shown by de' Servi. (Vestiges of old walls were found here in 1980, but not enough for clear identification.) Finally, at the corner of Friars' Lane and the Green we can see on the plan the corner tower shown by Wyngaerde and next to it what must be the banqueting house, branched out from the end of the galleries.

CRANE WHARF AND THE RIVERSIDE

The river in Tudor times was much wider in the area by the palace than it is today, but the waterline appears to have run back obliquely from what is now the end of Old Palace Lane to a point about 100 feet inside the present lawn of Trumpeters' House, then roughly parallel to the present riverbank to a point a little north of the bend in Friars' Lane and so across to Water Lane, well north of the White Cross pub. Our main witness for this is Wyngaerde. After the works of 1610–12 all was changed, and came much closer to the present waterline. There had been three islands by the palace, small and quite close inshore, which were absorbed into the river bank by 1612. Just where these islands were is unknown. The two tiny islets opposite the palace site today were part of a much larger island, which is probably where Richard II had his pavilion.

Recent work as part of an archaeological survey of the Thames riverbank has revealed timber posts in the water just off the end of Old Palace Lane which appear to be the supporting structures for a jetty and a landing stage. One timber was dated to 1584–85. This jetty and stage were no doubt built out from Crane Wharf. A crane was constructed at Shene between 1358 and 1361 in anticipation of Edward III's works. A crane on this site is depicted both in Moses Glover's map of Isleworth in 1635 and in Hollar's engraving of 1638. Whether a crane was there when Henry VII rebuilt the palace and continuously thereafter until the 1640's is unknown, but seems highly probable. It appears to have gone by 1653; no such machine is mentioned in a supplementary survey of Crane Piece compiled in that year.

THE LATEST ATTEMPT TO RECONSTRUCT THE PLAN OF THE TUDOR PALACE

Following the discovery of the de' Servi plan in 1998, Robert Cowie of the Museum of London Archaeological Service and I have made a further attempt to draw together all the evidence, archaeological, documentary, pictorial, to compile a revised plan of the Tudor Richmond Palace, superimposed on the modern Ordnance Survey plan of the area. The result should by now have been published, with all the supporting evidence, in the learned journal *Post-Mediaeval Archaeology*. Unfortunately the publication of our article has been held up until later in 2001. But the new plan itself is reproduced here.

The new plan of Richmond Palace

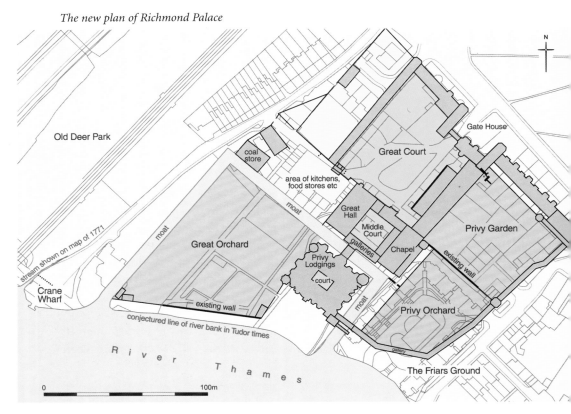

INDEX (illustrations in **bold** type)

LIST OF ILLUSTRATIONS AND ACKNOWLEDGEMENTS

Text © John Cloake, 2000
Published by the Richmond Local History Society, March 2001
Designed by Sally Lace Publishing Design
Printed by Watson & Crossland Ltd
Set in Adobe Minion 10.25/13.25pt
ISBN 0 9522099 6 9